DARK TALES
FROM THE DUNGEONS:

HORRORS FROM THE 'HOOD
FOR YOUTH TO BEWARE

A CONTRIBUTION FROM THE
MEN FOR HONOR WRITERS GROUP

PHILANTHROPY REQUEST

Ten percent of the proceeds of this book will be donated to PREP, a subsidiary of Office of Restorative Justice. These organizations prepare prisoners for release and promote public safety by ensuring that prisoners released from prison remain on a successful path toward re-entry to society. Readers are also encouraged to donate directly to PREP.

PREP

2049 S. SANTA FE AVENUE

LOS ANGELES, CA 90021

srmshodges@la-archdiocese.org

TABLE OF CONTENTS

INTRODUCTION, by Dortell Williams

This book is a collaboration of writings by The Men for Honor Writers Group at the California State Prison in Los Angeles County. This work – by prisoners serving time for non-violent drug offenses to first degree murder – offers diverse approaches to admonish, dissuade and advise youth how to avoid finding themselves in the horrific and tragic consequences of incarcerated life.

The Men for Honor Writers Group was borne out of The Honor Program, a pilot project that began in 2000 for programming prisoners who desire to change, reform themselves and grow as human beings. The Honor Program is the only one of its kind for men in California's labyrinth of thirty-three prison sites, and was officially sanctioned by the secretary of corrections, Matthew Cate, in 2009.

Since its inception, the men of the Men of Honor Program have saved taxpayers a pretty bundle of money by remaining racially riot free and refraining from the wholesale, typical inmate-on-inmate / inmate-on-staff violence that is of regular occurrence in maximum-security settings.

Eligibility for the program requires that prisoners be disciplinary free for five years, agree to random, mandatory drug testing and relinquish any former ties to gangs or hate groups. Prisoners must also participate in the many unique programs offered on the facility: peer education, multi-racial recreational activities, and hobby craft, along with consistent, general positive programming.

The Men for Honor Group is a peer-education collective. The concept is an outgrowth of the idea that prisoners with unique skills can teach others with the motivation and potential to hone the skill or art. Some peer education classes of note are: Prisoner Art Program, which teaches the fundamentals to art, from beginners drawing to high-end paintings that benefit charities and other needs in society. There is also a well numbered veterans group on the facility, as well as an academic educational group.

The Men for Honor group has been active – officially and unofficially – since 2005. Under the umbrella of peer education, the Men for Honor group has offered classes such as Spanish, Nutrition 101, Creative Thinking, Business class, HIV/AIDS Prevention and, of course, Creative Writing.

The mission statement of the Men for Honor Writing Group is: To promote a productive and peaceful environment of learning; utilizing our mutual skills to teach one another and build self-worth, life skills and gain a collective appreciation of one another.

With this collaborative work, we now extend our objectives of youth guidance, admonition, mentoring, crime *prevention* and philanthropy to the California community.

WHY GANG BANGING IS BAD FOR YOUNGSTERS

by DeAndre Griffin

I want to shout out from the rooftops; from the heights of the tallest buildings, from the crests of every mountain: YOUNGSTERS, BEWARE!

I wish I could say to every youngster who is looking to be accepted by a gang that you're looking in the wrong place, and for the wrong reasons, for acceptance. Acceptance is about being liked and appreciated because of who you are, not what the gang wants you to be. Acceptance is about being liked because of who you are inside, not what a gang can make you.

Gang banging was my life before I came to prison, so I can tell you by experience why this destructive activity is bad for upcoming youngsters. Gang banging takes us down generation after generation, we all meet the same life-destroying fates: prison, death, joblessness, ruin.

Gang banging is nothing to fool around with. It is a lifestyle of nonsense, ending all bad for its victims. Not only the victims you, as a gangbanger make, but you as a member become. That is the untold story about gang banging, it makes victims out of its hosts, then, when the gang banger is ruined and out of the way, it finds other hosts and does the same to them.

Gang banging destroys.

I once allowed my friends to choose me. After they got me in serious trouble – penitentiary trouble – then I realized they were really never my friends from the start. Anyone who doesn't care about your wellbeing, who does things to harm you in the name of fun, or pushes you to harm yourself, is no friend. Real friends want what's best for you, they really care about you.

So here I am sitting in a concrete cage in the penitentiary. I am alone; all alone and by myself. Yet I left a whole gang of homies out there. And they left me! Not a letter. Not a card. I can't even call them. I also left my family. I call home and when my dear mother is sick, I can't comfort her. My little brother is growing up without me; without my guidance and protection. My twin brother is doing his own thing, making it. I'm proud of him. But there's sadness in my heart because we used to do everything together. Now he's out there and I'm stuck in here. For what?

Joining a gang is a dead end choice. In prison, there are so many gang members it isn't funny. And the funny thing about it is that those same so-called enemies we shot at and hated so much on the streets are right in here with us; now we eat dinner together, play cards and basketball together, and get abused by the system together.

My former life as a gang member earned me a future of twenty-five years of heartache and misery in a human cage.

When you decide to gang bang you jeopardize your freedom and your life. You put yourself and your family at unnecessary risk. For what?

You see all of life's precious privileges go right down the drain. The fresh air; moving about in freedom without restraint; little things like ice cream cones and candy bars… gone. There are no girls in prison. Yeah, there's female staff, but they're off limits to us. They might as well not exist. Their very existence makes you feel bad; a constant reminder of all that you're missing.

Take it from an ex-gang member who feels the pain. Take it from a former gang banger who is a witness – over and over again – as to the misery the gang banging lifestyle leads to. A real and full life is about having choices. Gang banging steals choices away from you: from the colors you wear to who you can associate with and where.

A life without gang banging is a life with options. You don't need a gang to be cool or accepted. Think about it. The whole world accepts people from other parts of the world, but very few people outside of the underworld accept gang banging. Only gang bangers accept gang bangers. You don't have to follow others to be cool. Being cool is being accepted for who you are, for what you can do and offer.

Just like God made every day different, He also made every person different . God already sees you as divine and unique. But we have to see that uniqueness in ourselves. We have to explore our talents and abilities and then perfect them and share them with the world. That is what life is about, contributing positively to the world around us. Gang banging doesn't contribute to the world, it steals from it. Gang banging is negative. Living your life and contributing to it is positive.

Be the leader, and, perhaps the king you are destined to be. All you have to do is look within yourself and follow your heart. That's how we got Microsoft, Apple and, even, Ford automobiles. The founders of these great companies had a vision and they acted on it, not letting knuckle heads get in the way. We all have the potential. Man, you can be a leader by just being a good example. You can stay out of trouble and help your friends to stay out of trouble. You can be a hero by merely speaking up for what is right.

You can talk some sense into your friends and help them to realize that it's foolish to be out there gang bangin' and shooting over a street that nobody owns, has invested in, or will ever hold a piece of mortgage on.

Whoever you are youngster, take it from another youngster you'll likely never meet 'cause I'm locked away in here, stay away from gang bangin' and find the straight and narrow. That's the road you should be on and that's the road that will lead you to success.

KIDS: STAY OUT OF PRISON

by Bruce Benn

Kids! If there was ever a time to listen, now is that time. Lend your ears and listen to a man who tells not what he believes, or what someone else has told him, but what he has experienced himself. I am a prisoner. I live in a dreadful place. Day-in and day-out I am surrounded by concrete walls, steal cages and security glass.

Kids! Don't be like me. Be all that you can be with the positives out there. Don't do things that will send you to prison: drugs, stealing and robbing, disrespecting your parents and other elders. One thing that trips a lot of youngsters up is following others. There's an irony to this: you follow others, you do something stupid (I know, it seems cool at the time) and your so-called friends praise you for it -- like doing a beer run or something of that nature. Then when you get caught, and you eventually will, they won't even know you anymore.

The police put the handcuffs on you. You'll feel all alone; you are all alone. You're in the back of the police car and the police are taunting you, telling you that they are going to pin other crimes on you so you don't get out for a long, long time. Then you think about this page, right here, that you're reading right now, and how I warned you about this day. You think about the bad things that go on in that dark place called prison. How they take advantage of youngsters; how prisoners with mean faces, big tattoos and even bigger arms try to pressure you to do even stupider things. It is really rough.

Yeah, staying out of trouble seems easier said than done, but you should also know that making a one-second stupid decision could land you within a dreaded place called prison.

Imagine being in a cell just a few miles from home, but still separated by unforgiving walls. Now imagine being in a cell thousands of miles away, and having no contact with your family. Either way, you lose, and for what, a stupid decision? It is in this predicament that you learn who is really there for you. As the time fades with you being away, memories of you also fade. Friends forget about you and move on. Family has good intentions, but never seem to be there when you really need them. It's agonizing.

Right now it doesn't seem so bad, but that's because you are taking a lot for granted. You don't think about freedom of choice because you have it. You don't think about where you will live because you are in a home. You don't think about losing your family and friends because right now they are there. But just think: How do you feel about prisoners? When you go to jail that is exactly what you become – a prisoner -- and then people will feel the exact same way about you.

Right now you just want to be perceived as tough. You want others to think highly of you. And that is natural. But when you start doing stupid things for *their* approval then that's when things go all bad. Acting tough is not the same as having courage.

Acting tough is merely wearing a thin outer covering to hide what's inside. Courage is a noble trait that develops from within. Courage is genuine and can't be taken away by others. Yet courage is what you need to be yourself, to make people accept who you are; who you *really* are inside.

Listen, I'm saying all of this because I care. I don't want anyone to go through the crap I've gone through. I want you to live a better life than me. I want you to have a future, a real future with opportunities and success. I want you to see that there are paths to success and paths to destruction, and that the choice is yours.

So make wise and proper decisions. It's your life, don't throw it away.

GUM ON THE SIDEWALK

by Dortell Williams

Imagine this: I am locked in a cage, day and night. The four-walled, dry-gray concrete coffin I live in is about the size of your average bathroom, or closet. I must share it with another man. I peer from a window slat that is as wide as a small book, but as long as a broom handle. My "furniture," constructed of solid concrete, not unlike what you see in the Flintstones cartoons -- all snazzy and cool -- is non-descript and uncomfortable as all get out.

I get crooks in my neck at least once a month, the mattresses are as flat as French toast and the bunk itself is wafer thin. The guards set the temperature of the vent; a vent that blows recycled, stale air around and around the overcrowded housing unit. It seems they can never get it right. I'm not talking about Goldilocks here, just reasonable. In the winter you can expect cold air to blow in, in the summer you can bet the vents will be blowing hot air. That's just the way it is!

The yard space I am permitted to "roam" around in is about the size of your average neighborhood block, if not smaller. It is a dusty track and field with sparse grass and no trees. There's an asphalt roadway, but the only vehicles that pass it are ambulances – to carry the stabbing and slashing victims away.
The guards, many of them mean-spirited, tell me what I can eat, and what I can't. They tell me when I can use the phone, and when I can't. They tell me when I

can go outside, and when I can't. They stand by the food window and make sure you get no extras. They control the water in the shower – ten minutes! That's it. The guards read your mail coming in and going out. There is no privacy. They even strip search you and make you bend over so they can see where the sun don't shine. They use a flashlight to see.

Prison goes way beyond being grounded for a mere week and then when all is said and done you are forgiven – where there's reconciliation and you can go on like before. Prison is a never-ending life of being grounded. Even if you are one of the fortunate ones and you get a release date, your record is stained forever. People will judge you as if you had food on your face, or wore mismatched sox. Even after you fix yourself they still judge you. They will judge you – not for who you are, but for one act, for one mistake – forever and ever.

Such a life is not worthy for that of a dog, yet here I am – and thousands of others who thought they could get away from the system. Thousands of others who thought they would never get caught breaking the law. Yeah, some are innocent, but many are guilty. Once inside, it doesn't matter. You are society's trash, you're treated accordingly. Prison is society's trash bin; it is where the discarded are forgotten, forsaken.

You've heard about the food. Yep, it's as bad as they say it is. Most of it has no taste. There's never enough. They rush you to eat it. In like cattle and out like cattle; lines of men (or women) flow like rivers of ants. And like ants, from a distance, you can't tell one from the other. Certainly no one ant is better than another. They're all the same, and prisoners are no different. We wear the same clothes; there's no individuality in here.

Are your walls in your room decorated with posters and pictures and the like? Not in prison. The walls are as bland as the food, and the food is as bland as the walls. (Sometimes the food is as hard as the walls, too.)

Back in the day, many of us thought it was cool to ditch school, hang out and literally make nothing of ourselves. We thought we were so slick, getting away with this or that, then, it all caught up to us in one day, with one act.

A few new guys come in – tried and convicted – but impressed with their trial lawyers saying, "Man, I could have been a lawyer." Well, with a criminal record they'll never be one now! They mope down Lament Lane wishing they'd done things different. Some had others try to tell them to straighten up. They didn't listen. Others had no warning at all. They just fell into the pit of no return, stuck like a truck in the muck with the windows rolled up. No one can hear their cries; God scarcely hears their prayers 'cause many of them still haven't learned.

Prison is a lonely place. Oh, there's people around. It never stops. But real friendships are hard to find because prison is a dog-eat-dog world. The strong prey on the weak and the weak are chewed up and spit out. Have you ever heard of mercy? Well, she doesn't come here, and you shouldn't either!

If I were you, knowing what I know now, I'd stay in school, get good grades and build *yourself* for the future. I know it all sounds so square, but school is like a bank account. The more you put into it, the more you can withdraw when you finish. Prison is just the opposite. The longer you do, the more it drains you; saps you like a black widow caught in her web.

School offers opportunities and evens the playing field. If you're not attractive, your brains can take you where your looks can't – and vice versa. If you're not good at math then your way with words may cover for that weakness – and vice versa. If you're a person of detail, or can play an instrument, or know the sciences, life is begging for you to take it by the reins, but in prison there are no opportunities. Prison has no advantages to life. Prison is the place where life spits you out like gum.

Don't be like that chewed up wad of gum out there on the sidewalk; stepped on and disrespected. Be the shoes that step on that gum! Prison ain't nothin' but a place where there's a whole lot of gum on the sidewalk.

Something No One Told Us About Selling Drugs

by DeAundre Bowman

I started selling drugs at the age of ten. Everyone on my block was infatuated with the hustle of crack in the mid-'80s. Being so young, basically a child, I was easily influenced by my older homies. As long as we weren't using the dope it seemed harmless.

As I got older, started having money, and experiencing some independence, I found myself being more rebellious toward my family. I felt I could take care of myself, I didn't need any help. At the age of about fourteen I was completely out of control: I was running away from home, postin' up in dope spots to make money, and you couldn't tell me anything. Because of the way I was trippin', my mother asked me, "Boy, is you smokin' crack?" I wasn't, but I might as well have been. I was really acting up. I didn't care about anything or anybody – only my money.

It got to the point where I was shootin' at other dudes, breakin' into homes and trading their goods for bud and other drugs. I'm tellin' you, I was a wild boy.

As the years went on I found myself in and out of juvenile hall -- quickly making my way to youth authority. I got busted for possession of a firearm; breaking and entering; strong-armed robberies, and violating parole. I had a real problem with authority. "Don't tell me what to do," was my attitude. Stint after stint in confinement – I hated it! Guards telling me to go "Lock it up," meaning for me to go in my cage. I was deprived of the most basic things: like going to the refrigerator whenever I wanted; or taking a shower after a day's activities; or talking on the phone when I wanted, for as long as I wanted to. And yet all I could think about was how I was going to boost my hustle once I hit the block again. I was just like a junkie, stuck in thought about the next fix. My fix was the fast money.

Once I got out of youth authority, my hustle was stronger than ever. I thought I was really slick. I never caught a drug case. I could cook the drugs like a real chemist, and I kept crack by the ounces, making sure that I made at least $2,000 a day. When I failed to make my quota I turned into an irritable beast.

One time I was so short I hit my connection. I waited for him around one o'clock (Yep, right in the middle of the day!) When he showed up I hit'em for like eight ounces of dope. I became heartless over time, hurting more people, even pimping for money.

On another occasion I was on E-status, pockets held nothing but lint … and a pistol. A Jamaican was chipped up with his woman at a taco shop with a drive-thru. I quietly stood behind the scenes and peeped them out. She was curvy, blonde hair, short. He was thin as a pipe, tryin' to pop it and mackin' like it was going out of style. The Jamaican was bejeweled in diamonds and decked in suede, I made up my mind to rob him. He wore a billboard on his forehead that pretty much said he was harmless as a butterfly, and had not a lick of flavor to his style.

As he made his order, I made my move. I signaled to my boys who worked inside to turn to the blind as I pushed forward. Before he knew it I was in his face, my hand was through his car window and my pistol was pointed between his dark, bulging eyes. I ordered him to empty his pockets. He followed my instructions flawlessly, but as I went for his car his girl refused to unlock the door. I popped the Jamaican upside his head a few times and that did the trick. The delay made me mad so I stripped him down to his boxers. (I know, I did him bad.) And what was my motive? Money.

I didn't have to be a drug user to destroy my life. Drugs have that effect either way it goes. Get involved with them and watch your life go down the drain. I thought I was special, different. I didn't think anything could happen to me. It's funny but sad. There are thousands and thousands of people in prison who probably thought the same thing.

By the time I stopped to realize what I was doing it was too late. I was sentenced to two terms of life without the possibility of parole, three terms of life with the possibility of parole, plus twenty years as a consequence to a neighborhood drug war.

The moral of this story is that drugs are just as addictive to both buyer and seller and equally destructive. The many nights I stayed up laughing and gleefully counting the piles of money I had accumulated have now turned into never- ending nights of calculating all the years of prison I owe, but will never complete in a life time.

THINK *BEFORE* YOU ACT
by Willie Baker

Most of us learn the value of currency at an early age. From that time on we do our very best to do what is necessary to gain it and keep it. Some people get honest jobs, whatever that may entail. Others go rogue and selfishly rob and steal from others: either by gun point or with a deceptive pen.

As up and coming youth, here are some questions you might ask yourself as you consider your own ways and means:

- Does what you do bring you sadness or joy, embarrassment or pride?
- Would the consequences be negative or positive?
- How could this activity impact my family?
- Is this what I want for my family?

Life within itself has enough horror, shame and uncertainty. And that is a life led by honest living.

Now, just think about the one friend you know or who you've heard of who went to juvenile hall. Surely he was frightened to wit's end. His family was shamed under the table. And neither he nor his family knows what will happen to him as the chapters slowly turn forward.

It doesn't sound like an appealing personal story, does it?

The alternative to this type of life, a life full of horror, shame and uncertainty is to go straight, and keep it clean. Get educated, find a job and live a more secure and stable life. Where's the shame in that? Last I heard these were good aims; respectable, noble, peaceful. This is the stuff a wonderful family life is made of.

On the other hand, a life of drugs or alcohol can lead you to the end, before you even started in life. That is what juvenile hall is: an end before the beginning. Not to say that one should throw in the towel if he does land in juvee. But having to start any race by first having to climb out of the hole to get to the starting line is a backward beginning, do you agree?

Life is hard enough on the straight and narrow. It's hard enough trying to do it right from the get-go. My warning to you is don't make it that much harder by starting off in the hole and thinking you can just come up any time you want. It doesn't work like that. Never has, never will.

So my message to you young men and women out there thinking you can come up right quick, or cheat your way through life by messing over others is: Think *before* you act! Otherwise it could be too late.

THE LAB RAT LIFE
by Leonard Russell

If I was in a complaining mood (and obviously I am) I would complain about some of these guards with chips on their shoulders. No one likes bullies or people who think they're all that, but that's what we have to deal with as prisoners. As prisoners we have it hard enough without these guards coming in and rubbing it in our face. They think they are better than us because they have a job (and rule over us) and we are in prison (*for* them to rule over us).

The bottom line is that we made bad decisions and that's what put us in prison. So now we're in this situation where we must rely on them for everything. I mean everything. We have to rely on them to send our letters out, or to deliver letters from our people to us. We have to rely on them to give us job assignments or let us use the phone, or even shower. We have to rely on them to feed us, man! I mean everything is dependent on them.

Have you ever felt like a lab rat? I'll bet you've never been asked that question before. But it is one you might think about. We feel like lab rats sometimes. Today the guards want to try making us go to breakfast early. Tomorrow they want to try making us go late. Today they want to see how we respond if they change the rules – without warning. Tomorrow everything is smooth. Each day we must rely on them to run some type of program, if they run program at all.

Living in a small cage with another man is like being a lab rat, too. One guy paces the floor – back and forth, back and forth. If he were a hamster he'd be on the spinning wheel going around and around, yet going absolutely nowhere. That description represents the whole prison experience. I call it the lab rat life.

I am a grown man, but I have guards younger than me telling me what to do. It makes me feel less than human. It makes me feel like I'm being baby sat. It makes me feel like the guards have got their foot on my neck.

No matter how good you are, no matter how much you strive to stay out of trouble, you are not rewarded for your efforts. This is no way to be treated. If I could tell every youngster in the world not to come to prison I would. I would tell them: Don't come to prison because if you do, they'll treat you like a lab rat!

THERE ARE NO DIFFERENCES BETWEEN US

by Zachariah Barrow

We boys all covet the same things in life. We admired the elders in our life who we watched from a distance. We imagined ourselves in their shoes one day, with the nice clothes and shiny rides. We wanted the women and everything else that comes with the fast life. Without direction, meandering minds are a playground for the curious and a place for evil seeds to mature.

I was sent to the California Youth Authority at a very young age. My crime? It was my attitude: rebellious and therefore uneducated. Sure, there will always be reasons for why we do the things we do. But are they good reasons? We are always looking for a means to an end, but is it a good means to a good end? Locked up as an adult I now must reflect what my reasons where, what my means to my ends were. It's all about motivation. What motivates you? What motivates me?

I wanted the easy life. I wanted to live comfortable, not struggling to pay bills like others in my family. Doing crime was the easy way to get a quick few bucks in my pocket. What was missing was my understanding of the consequences. Sure, I knew I could get in trouble. But who would ever imagine getting twenty-five years for stealing pizza? Those are some heavy consequences. Then there's the faulty thinking that "I can get away with it." I lied to myself. You know the spiel: "I won't get caught"; "Just this one time," and et cetera. Lies, lies and more lies.

The truth is, once you compromise and get involved with crime you get addicted to it. The rush you get from trying to go undetected. You get a thrill from getting something for nothing; the challenge of planning the move and getting away with it. It is addictive. Crime becomes your drug. You need it; you have to have that fix!

This might all sound crazy, but it's true. Crime will control you like a drug. The power of it makes you think differently. It changes who you are inside. Crime dictates who you are, and what you are. It makes you a shell, an empty shell; searing your conscience.

I imagine you are a generation younger than me. Life changes with each generation. But human nature remains the same. My generation said it all before your generation. And now my generation is living the consequences. That is why I'm writing this to you. I didn't have this warning. The elders I referred to at the start of this piece were bad examples for me. They weren't heroes or role models. They were bad actors, simple as that. And I followed them.

Now I'm here to tell you to think about the consequences. Ask yourself what it is worth? If you're tempted to steal a car, ask yourself what it is worth? I mean, think on this: If you work for a year, and save, maybe you can get a really nice used car. Or perhaps you can put a down payment on a new car. But if you steal a car and happen to get caught you'll do a lot longer than one year in the joint.

If you're sent away to prison then there are more consequences. Would you be able to stand missing your family for years at a time? Would your girlfriend stick with you? (She'd probably be ashamed of you.) Do you enjoy your freedom on the streets, being able to do what you want, when you want? All of that is gone on the inside. No more walking on the beaches with bare feet and ice pops melting under the luxuriant sun. Do you love Fido, or Lil' kitty? Well, in prison you can just forget about them. They might not live by the time you get out.

And if you said yes to any of these questions then I now know you've given some thought to doing time behind these walls.

Learn from the mistakes of others and you'll never have to suffer as they do.

Prison means confinement. Prisoners are the confined. But you can also be confined in your own mind by accepting the limitations others put on you. Others may tell you that you'd be a good gang member, but what about all the other things you could be good at? Still, others may tell you that you'd only be good at hands on work, but even that's too confining. You'd actually be good at whatever you enjoy and think you'd be good at. You're a uniquely made individual with your own voice, finger prints, face and DNA. You can be whoever and whatever you work toward being.

In the 'hood, back in the day, it was easy to stick a gun in someone's face and take their belongings. But a real man cherishes his life, his freedom and is proud to live a prosperous life he can be proud of without constantly having to look over his shoulders for the gang of enemies he's made jacking and dogging people.

You're an individual. You think like an individual. You live your own individual life. So why would you want to throw away all of that individuality only to become a nameless, faceless run-of-the-mill inmate?

Pick up a book and read, study, be productive and constructive. This way you'll stay out of prison, you'll be happy and be different from people like me.

DON'T IGNORE THIS MESSAGE
by Drew Williams

I wish I could give every youngster in the world some advice. Advice that would keep them from the hell and heartache I've been through; advice that would lead them towards a more fruitful and happy life; a life of contentment and satisfaction; instead of a life of misery, pain and deprivation.

For you youth I can reach with these immediate words:

Don't ignore this message:

Youth, you are young, supple and full of positive potential; don't take your age for granted. Don't be out drinking your life away like the bums you see on the street with their green wino bottles. Don't be out there smoking weed, missing school and getting arrested. I know you think it can't happen to you, but it happens all the time. Why not you? It's happening to so many others.

Stay in school, where you belong. Schools were made for youth, and that is where you should be. Otherwise society would have you in some factory working twelve hours a day like in the early years of America before they figured out school was better for kids.

Don't think just because you're young doesn't mean that bad things can't happen to you when you do wrong. Surely you've heard about some of your peers in your age group getting life imprisonment or even the death penalty. It happened to them, it could happen to you. How would you feel if you got life in prison? Could you imagine how it would feel if you got the death penalty?

I hope neither of these disasters happen to you. And the best way to prevent them from happening to you is to avoid doing the things that can lead to these types of sentences.

It is a lot easier than you think. You just want to do a minor lick; snatch a purse let's say. So you snatch and run. The old lady you victimize is suddenly stricken with fear and dies of a heart attack right there on the spot. Guess what? You get the murder. Of course you didn't mean for that to happen. Of course that wasn't part of the plan. But it did happen and they charge you with the rap. For you it *is* a wrap!

Don't let your friends lead you to a dead end. They try to tell you it's cool to do this or that … and you know it isn't. But you want to fit in. Follow your first mind and do what is right. Don't worry about disappointing them because I can guarantee you, if you listen to them it's your family that will be disappointed.

Don't drop out of school. That is the worst thing you can do. Are you a quitter? Are you a loser? That is what you would be if you quit school and lost all of the opportunities that an education brings. Get the best education you can. Even if the teacher doesn't teach anything, there are always books. Read them yourself; learn to teach yourself. The better your education, the less likely you'll find yourself in circumstances where you need to snatch a purse or something stupid like that. First, you'll be too busy for that type of stuff. Second, you'll have enough money to give to old ladies instead of taking from them.

Don't run before you can walk. Take each day in its place and don't worry about weeks, months or years from now. Do what you need to do for today, for the present. Life has stages. That's why youth go to school first, and then work. Don't try to obtain too much before your time. Some people work for years – and stay out of prison – before they buy that nice home, Benz or Porsche. (If it is these that are in your sights.)

Whatever you do, don't ignore this message!

A WRONG TURN IN THE FORK IN THE ROAD

by Drew Williams

I am a forty-eight-year-old man who's been locked up over half of my life. Selfish activities such as robbery, selling drugs, and violent acts got me a life sentence.

I started robbing and stealing at a young age – twelve-years-old. I used to hang out with so-called friends all day and into the night. We had mischief on our minds: perhaps breaking into a storefront, robbing some mark or whatever we could get into. By the time I turned thirteen I had been to juvenile hall two times; both for a short stay. Did I learn from that? Not hardly. These experiences in the mini-clink were but a horrible omen for what was to come.

My parents would try to warn me, "If you don't stop what you're doing they're going to lock you up and throw away the key." I'd tell them that I wouldn't rob or steal anymore, but then I got into selling weed to my neighborhood peers. I knew I was headed towards a wreck; I knew I was softly careening off course and into a horrible smash up.

One day the weed sales led me into an assault with a deadly weapon. I didn't see the assault coming, and the victim didn't see me coming. It just happened. I was shipped back to juvenile hall and then on to the California Youth Authority, where short stays turn into long stays real quick. That is but a brief description of my teen years. Years lost in the fog of mindlessness, years that I can't redeem or get back.

I have lived the most troubled life you could ever imagine, it was a journey I chose; a road I willingly walked; a path I picked. From the age of thirteen until I was seventeen I saw nothing but concrete floors and barred doors. It isn't a life I would recommend for anyone, not even a worst enemy. Yet, it was a life I walked right into, not by words, not by a multiple choice sheet of paper, not by a raffle, but by actions.

At seventeen, just released from the joint, I thought I was all that. I had lived the hard-knock life and survived to see another day of freedom. But did I learn? Not hardly. I got right back on the expressway towards destruction. Though I didn't see it then, I was living out that life my parents had warned me about. By my eighteenth birthday I was in the county jail, but this time I was on my way to the big house. At that point I could see my life swirling towards the drain, going down, down, down.

It was in prison where the real violence entered my life. Stab or be stabbed. So I picked up a knife and left my mark, while others left their marks on me. I learned quickly that I was around people who didn't play games. The guards carried guns and the prisoners carried knives. The future was very bleak.

From twelve years of age until my thirties I was in and out of jail; back and forth. I had become what they call a recidivist. I was in a vicious cycle of street life, prison life, street life and more prison life. At age thirty the judges, the juries … society, had had it. A hammer came swinging down silently over my existence and when that bad boy landed it sent shock waves through my life that I am still reeling over.

They showed me the key, right there in the courtroom. The judge, the jury and society. It was a shiny key, with a full bright future attached to it, and a nice dose of hope. After they let me examine it for a minute from a distance, they tossed it, far, far away from my grasps. I watched it disappear into the distant darkness clinking and clanging farther and farther away until it was all together gone. My parents were right: they had locked me up and thrown away the key.

This might sound like a nightmare, but it is my life. This is my story. I am writing in hopes that you won't make it your story, too. If you are on a road towards destruction: Stop! Don't watch as you careen towards the crash and do nothing like I did. To be honest, looking back, it wasn't even a fun ride.

I threw years away. I tossed my life away. The real nightmare in all of this is that it was really me who threw those keys away. I made the choice with my actions long before the judge and the juries and society got involved.

I encourage you with my all to stay in school and get your education. You could be the next Bill Gates or Tyra Banks ... or even the next President of the United States! With the right education anything is possible. Stay in school; and not only that, listen to your parents. They care for you.

34

A LIST OF THINGS TO THINK ABOUT

by Lase Funches

Below are common experiences we prisoners face, year after year; after freakin' year. It is written to provoke thought for those of you messin' around out there and headed this way, to prison, to doing time, to, perhaps, being my neighbor. Think about this:

Would you be mad if…?

1. your toilet went out on Thursday and they wouldn't come fix it until
     Tuesday … or "maybe" Wednesday?

2. your power went out Thursday and they wouldn't come fix it until
     Tuesday … or "maybe" Wednesday?

3. they keep you locked up in your cage for 365 days on lockdown?

4. you have no choice in the menu, or what time you eat. The food tastes like nothing 'cause it has no taste.

5. you aren't allowed a shower for three or four days because of lockdowns, even though the shower is empty and just eight steps away.

6. you don't get clean sheets and towels weekly like you're supposed to.

7. you are told what to do, when to do it and how fast to do it even though it doesn't make you a better person, nor make any sense.

8. you had a legitimate complaint and no one cared.

9. you get sick and no one cares or helps you.

10. the guards wake you up at night by beating on the door or window to "make sure you're alive."

The list goes on and on; it is vast. This is prison; you lose your right to be human when you're sent here. Being in prison is like being stuck in a nightmare that never ends, and you never awaken. Yet you feel everything; everything is real: the stench, the pain, the misery, the loneliness, the regret. It all gangs up on you to grip you, grab you and shake you up every minute, every day, every second of your life.

Prison breaks your communication with the world you knew and loved so dearly. Friends disappear: poof! They're just gone. Cherished possessions seem to just gain feet and walk away. Mail screeches to an abandoning halt. Even worse are all the letters telling you how much fun you're missing out on.

Life in prison is no life at all. Prison really isn't for human beings, and when they put you in prison your humanity fades every time you hear the echo of that deafening cage door slam.

BEHIND THE MASK
OF A DRUG DEALER

by Delmar Dixon

Behind the mask of a drug dealer is a lost soul. To live a life of crime is to live without reason. Why kill for the right to sell on a concrete corner when you are only passing through? Death is permanent, and so is its damage.

I see more people in prison, with me, for drugs than anything else. Drugs are addictive – for buyer and seller. So don't waste your younger years in foolishness that will get you nowhere worthwhile. Invest in yourself, invest in your future and always have something to be proud of from there on.

When we're young and trying to figure out the complexities of this confusing life we often see the world as the enemy. Our characteristics reveal that of a thug -- thinking only of ourselves, thinking the world owes us something. It does not.

Everything is by choice and we chose our beginning and our ending, for better or for worse. Don't do dumb and dumb won't betray you, she won't even know you.

Many of us from the game lived the lives of those before us. I know I did; and ended up in the same wretched place as those that preceded me. My advice to you is to live *your* life, not theirs. Figure out what you are good at, what your talent might be and pursue that with gusto.

Don't be a lost soul.

Don't live a life of hurt, pain and fear.

A NIGHTMARE OF 25-YEARS TO LIFE

by Ivory L. Downs

I was sentenced to twenty-five years to life. At first it seemed like a nightmare. I kept waking up to this hellhole hoping it was a nightmare, hoping I would wake up from this … reality. Finally, after three long years, I have finally come to terms with the reality of my sentence. My sentence is every bit as real as I am in the flesh. This, I regret, is real life – and I'm stuck in it.

Looking back I can confidently say there are a lot of things I would do differently if I had the chance. I did some pretty senseless and stupid things to get in here and now I would do just about anything to get out. I want my freedom back! For now, I must endure. I must put up with every detail of life that accompanies being a prisoner, including:

- being told when to shower (no matter how clean or dirty I am)
- making sweatshop wages, and valued a lot less in attitude by the guards
- being subject to strip searches – every day
- being degraded by a constant lack of privacy – even to use the bathroom
- being forced to lay in the rain, dirt or mud every time an alarm goes off
- seeing females (guards, nurses, doctors) but prohibited from befriending them

All of these things, and so much more, are daily reminders of the decision I willfully made to put myself in here. If I could help anyone avoid making the same mistakes I did to come here, I would.

I would tell those with anger issues to get help, talk to someone. Uncontrolled anger led me straight to the gray gates of hell and the heat of the place comes from within as you stew in your stupidity and steam in regret.

It is a fact that the emotion of anger is a dangerous characteristic that leads a lot of people to make drastic and dire mistakes. I've since learned to deal with my anger by allowing a cooling off period before taking action. By allowing time to pass you help yourself to get in a mind frame to make sound judgment. You can actually stop and think about the consequences when your "madness" has eased (which originally meant crazy, by the way).

It is important to guard and protect your future by thinking of the consequences, by not acting irrationally and by being responsible – even when upset. Sometimes the best people to give advice are those who've made the most or worst mistakes. If you listen to us you don't have to repeat the mistakes we did. My advice would be a quote from NBC's Chris Mathews, "Don't get mad; don't get even, get ahead!"

Don't lose your temper, collect it, and fuel that energy into great things.

A CAGE AND NEW FRIENDS

by Travon Pugh

Prison isn't where I thought I'd be ten years ago. Never did I imagine that I would be wrapped up within a cage of bars pretty much as tight as the skin on a drum. Yet here I am.

My life was supposed to be better than this. Better than a hopeless life sentence. If it were not for the friends prison gives you, as you walk into those wide, gray creaking and clanking doors, I'd be lonelier than ever, but thanks to the generosity of prison I get to kick it with Misery, Isolation and Confinement. These are my new friends; oh, along with Dread.

Misery reminds me of why this place is so dreadful. They are actually twins. Misery is the first cousin of Loneliness and in spite of all these new friends, if I erase the good face, I couldn't be any more lonely.

I am isolated from the world I knew and grew up in for all of my young life. I am confined to a concrete and steel cage no bigger than the average bathroom. I am locked under a key that other people control twenty one hours a day. I am allowed the bare necessities. That's why it is dreadful, or, *full* of dread; however you want to put it.

Youngins, this is just a couple of pages of a long and dread-filled book of lament I could share with you;

things that you, too, would quickly come to know if you chose to subject yourselves to criminal activities.

I can't say I didn't have someone to tell me what I am now telling you. I did. I just chose not to listen. I let everything they preached (which is what I called it) go in one ear and right out the other.

Don't be like me. You don't need friends like mine.

DON'T BE A LOSER

by Travon Pugh

Now caged like an animal, my actions let my mama down, tremendously. For she wasn't just hoping, but expecting me to accept the college football scholarship I was offered. Just think how much different my life could have been, for me, and everyone who knows me. My selfishness caused more hurt than I could have ever imagined. My selfishness actually hurt my mama more than it hurt me, because I love her so dearly.

My mama invested a lot in me. She bred me to be successful and showed me many avenues toward a fulfilling path. She had hopes of me being the pride of my family, knowing that I had the potential. My mama gave me the air and space to spread my wings and take on the world.

Instead, I chose to smoke weed, join a gang; I took my eyes off the prize. Already floating on my potential, I came crash landing inside perpetual electrified walls that I can't seem to find my way out of.

My mistakes were made in my youth. Most mistakes are made when we are young and inexperienced. When we refuse to listen to the advice of the people who have already been where we're trying to go. As today's youth, your lives are the most valuable possessions in all of existence.

Think of how unique you are: your voice is uniquely yours. No one has your finger prints. And who could mimic your DNA? Your face is personal and your mannerisms, your very character is uniquely you. So make the best of your uniqueness and make a positive impact on the world. Listen to your parents, your teachers and all the other positive people who live in your community. They are your heroes, not the illusions you see on TV or in sports or depicted as so-called celebrities.

Listen to me, a prime example of a failed human specimen, a prisoner, a loser.

LETTER TO MY FAMILY MEMBER
by Lester Polk

As I write this letter from the steel cage within which I now reside, I can't help but remember the many admonitions and warnings that predicted my present fate. Unfortunately, I was too proud, too blind and too busy doing *my* thing to care.

Now I find myself in an embarrassing predicament, shamed because I gave up my future and all of my inherent potential for a very short, unfulfilling, vain lifestyle. I am embarrassed because all of you who loved me; all of you who consistently warned me; all of you who bent over backwards to open my eyes, yet failed to reach me because I had already fortified my personal space with walls.

You tried with all of your might to get me to see that my choices would lead to destruction, but your wisdom sounded foolish to me. In my demented thinking, I thought my potential could be fulfilled in the streets. I was chasing that which was unholy; seeking to fill a void that only God could fulfill.

I thought I wanted money, but to this day I can't tell you what I thought money would do for me. I thought I wanted respect, but I can't say that I truly knew the definition of the word.

I remember when the entire family came together to try to reason with me.

You all pleaded with me to change. In response, I tried to an extent, but found myself powerless and without the mindset to do so. My failure only hardened me towards the street lifestyle.

As a result of my misdirection, I now find myself caged like an animal; left with only fleeting memories of the so-called good times. For me, those good times were times of vanity, misdirection and wasted time. Now I find myself in a completely different set of times *and* circumstances.

Gone are the compassionate embraces and surroundings of family. These precious interactions and ambience are now replaced by the very harsh realities of prison life: of anti-social behavior, distrust and treachery in a completely compassionless, cut-throat, concrete jungle where the rules of civility are left outside of the prison's entrance.

Instead of the soft, kind words of loved ones, there is a constant and deafening drip of condemnation and condescension from my captors. In my world, the heart-aching separation of family, the chilling clank of closing gates and the eternally unforgiving walls that daily surround me are enough of a reminder of the consequences of my bad decisions. It seems, at least to me, that their biggest mission is to further remind me of my lost former life and wasted dreams; along with the trauma of being arrested.

In my former life I could not hear my family's life-saving words to me. I could not see the valuable road towards redemption that they tried so hard to place before me. Now it seems my hearing and sight could not be any more clear as the guards jack-hammer their cackles in my ears and point their lasers in my sights.

The paradox is how such a hard place could so liberally give understanding. Now, here, deep within the belly of the beast, I use my new found insight to call out to God – the author of all life.

Now I realize the extent of my rebellion; how I hated direction and my heart despised correction. I disobeyed the voice of my teachers and failed to incline my ears towards those with instruction. I was on the verge of total ruin, yet in the midst of the pure assembly (tailored from Proverbs 5:12-14).

So what does all of that mean to you, my young reader? What does it mean to you that I sit here rotting away, destroyed to a degree and put away? What it means is that I made a grave mistake; a mistake that you do not have to repeat.

I did not listen until it was too late, but it is not too late for you to listen; to become the person who you were created to be. But for that you'll have to plug into your creator.

You might say that you are not a religious person. And that's fine. But I know you are a smart and wise person, if no other reason than that you are reading this book. (Plus, only fools say no to God {Smile} (Psalms 14:1)

My transformation was made after I turned to the Lord. If you desire to have a better life; a life of change and transformation; a life with hope of an eternal, spiritual future, you too, can call upon the Lord. Just talk to Him, tell Him you want to change your life and you want Him to help you. Seek others who believe in Jesus and read the Bible yourself.

Even in prison, I'm happy I did.

PART II: POETRY SECTION

Lost
by Leonard Russell

lost without a cause

helpless, fearful, lost

memories, prison's graveyard.

trouble, some kid egoless,

heart clutched inside black

vortex!

bars wrapped around bodies

triggerless mind frame

steel cages, beatless hearts.

lost.

THE PATH

by Delmar Dixon

To live a good and healthy life, live
define the path
take it, walk it.

Avoid street life
like the ebb & flow of traffic
losses, wins and losses rise & fall;
street lights blacken, leaving light void
family members fade from memory
grey walls, riots, bland like Gerber.

TV's soft illusion,
reality's hard lessons – for life!
too short for life in bars, cages;
too long for sentences of life
Avoid street life

CURIOUS FEATHERED FRIEND
by Dortell Williams

Dull gray feathers; peering eyes ... curious

gazing thru a three-inch window slat, tier two ... so curious

hovering thoughts, silent bubble above -- like a comic:

What are you doing in there?

Won't you come play with me?

tiny gray head twitches up, down, s
                                    i
                                   d
                                    e
                                     w
                                      a
                                     y
                                       s ...ever so
curious

looking, peering, gazing at the human in a cage – still curious

glazed onyx eyes, bright, communicating sorrow, cognizant of the amiss

little feet balance like miniature stilts, dance and prance, desperate offer of help a chirp and a ½ = helplessness; two = completely forlorn

from a distance two can't be heard, forlorn the feathers flew

weird, weird world where birds peer in on people; caged

unanswered questions leave, fly away – forlorn

still curious.

RAW AND STRAIGHT
By Phillip Black

check it out!

Raw and Straight!

life is short

you only have 1

live & b free

love your mother

love your father

you have 1 ea.

listen to them

you have 2 ears

to not listen is …

looong misery

To not listen to them could mean a looong journey with strangers behind bars listening to uniformed people, who do not love, like or respect you.

Raw and Straight!

NOTES TO PARENTS

A FALLEN CHILD IS SOCIETY'S FALL
by Mechi Gleason

To sit and watch a precious child fall by the way side is a horrifying sight. The waste of a child, not a weed, but a small and potentially glorious human being, is tragic. Yet kids are falling prey to a crooked and corrupted society, daily; falling like felled trees en masse, but silently.

Also silent is a world of people, loud in violence, with a watching society either too busy or apathetic to intervene. Too many of us are possessed by the notion that if it isn't our child then it's none of our business. But it is that neglected child that does society harm: getting involved in crime, adding to the victim's roster, not contributing as adults and perhaps, in the worst case scenario, stirring an enormous drain on state coffers as an idle and warehoused inmate.

If you see a child going astray, lend a hand, provide sound advice, and lead her in the right direction. It may be you who has the right words, the advantageous timing or the perfect position to make the difference. In this adverse world where so many elements in our culture are against our youth, society needs you to intervene, give a child a chance and create an opportunity where none before existed.

If our children fall, so does our future. Truly, a child's fall is society's fall.

CONVINCING THE CHILDREN THAT PRISON IS NOT WHERE THEY WANT TO BE

by Bruce Benn

In ancient times Jesus was asked who is the greatest in the kingdom of heaven. "And Jesus called a little child unto him, and set him in the midst of them and said: 'Verily I say unto you, except you be converted and become as little children, ye shall not enter into the kingdom of heaven. Whoever shall therefore humble himself as this little child, the same is the greatest in the kingdom of heaven.'"*

The example given signifies the purity and simplicity of the child. In speech, in action, they are pure; they tell truth as it is seen and absorbed by them. If one is short, or fat, or even if one stinks of odor, a child will innocently and with all good intention blurt the truth out.

Yet we allow them to be contaminated by society, through the media and a corrupted culture. There are hardly any filters left for a child's mind. As parents, as neighbors and teachers, we must collectively be a filter, that genuine source of guidance that every child needs to continue in that state of innocence.

In an age where society now charges children as adults for mistakes, and punishes them with adult consequences, we must protect them. Protect them from the harmful, life-destroying influences of the world; from the rampant corruption that so insidiously contaminates them as youth.

Gold is a precious commodity because, as investors, we expect for gold to increase in value, to mature and yield for us a better future. Yet children are so much greater in value than gold. Whatever precious seed we plant in them can bloom into unfathomable potential. At the risk of sounding cliché, children truly are our future. Borrowing a line from singer Whitney Houston, a rich point is made: "We must teach them well and allow them to lead the way."

Parents, the elders, the community must teach and guide our youth. It is a joint effort. We must constantly counter the negative influences that they are faced with on a daily basis. We must prioritize schooling for the children, and not second rate education, either; compromised by pork barrel expenditures and later, failed prison policies *after* we've allowed them to go astray.

Perhaps these ingredients might help retain that beautiful, natural disposition that Jesus spoke of in the Scriptures. It's not up to them; it's first up to us.

Sources:

*New Kings James Version, Nelson's Study Bible (Thomas Nelson, Inc., Nashville, TN, 1982): pp. 1606, 1607

King James Version, Key Word Study Bible (AMG Publishers, Chattanooga, TN, 1991): p. 1206

A portion of the proceeds for this project will be

directed at various charities in the community.

Thank you for your support.

www.ingramcontent.com/pod-product-compliance
Lightning Source LLC
Chambersburg PA
CBHW070822290526
45795CB00002B/807